Iter Carolinum being a succinct relation of the necessitated marches, retreats, and sufferings, of His Majesty Charls the I from January 10, 1641, till the time of his death 1648 (1660)

Edward Walker

Iter Carolinum being a succinct relation of the necessitated marches, retreats, and sufferings, of His Majesty Charls the I from January 10, 1641, till the time of his death 1648
Walker, Edward, Sir, 1612-1677.
Preface signed: Thomas Manley.
Attributed to Edward Walker. Cf. Halkett & Laing (2nd ed.).
[4], 32 p.
London : Printed by W. Godbid ..., 1660.
Wing / W339
English
Reproduction of the original in the Henry E. Huntington Library and Art Gallery

Early English Books Online (EEBO) Editions

Imagine holding history in your hands.

Now you can. Digitally preserved and previously accessible only through libraries as Early English Books Online, this rare material is now available in single print editions. Thousands of books written between 1475 and 1700 and ranging from religion to astronomy, medicine to music, can be delivered to your doorstep in individual volumes of high-quality historical reproductions.

We have been compiling these historic treasures for more than 70 years. Long before such a thing as "digital" even existed, ProQuest founder Eugene Power began the noble task of preserving the British Museum's collection on microfilm. He then sought out other rare and endangered titles, providing unparalleled access to these works and collaborating with the world's top academic institutions to make them widely available for the first time. This project furthers that original vision.

These texts have now made the full journey -- from their original printing-press versions available only in rare-book rooms to online library access to new single volumes made possible by the partnership between artifact preservation and modern printing technology. A portion of the proceeds from every book sold supports the libraries and institutions that made this collection possible, and that still work to preserve these invaluable treasures passed down through time.

This is history, traveling through time since the dawn of printing to your own personal library.

Initial Proquest EEBO Print Editions collections include:

Early Literature

This comprehensive collection begins with the famous Elizabethan Era that saw such literary giants as Chaucer, Shakespeare and Marlowe, as well as the introduction of the sonnet. Traveling through Jacobean and Restoration literature, the highlight of this series is the Pollard and Redgrave 1475-1640 selection of the rarest works from the English Renaissance.

Early Documents of World History

This collection combines early English perspectives on world history with documentation of Parliament records, royal decrees and military documents that reveal the delicate balance of Church and State in early English government. For social historians, almanacs and calendars offer insight into daily life of common citizens. This exhaustively complete series presents a thorough picture of history through the English Civil War.

Historical Almanacs

Historically, almanacs served a variety of purposes from the more practical, such as planting and harvesting crops and plotting nautical routes, to predicting the future through the movements of the stars. This collection provides a wide range of consecutive years of "almanacks" and calendars that depict a vast array of everyday life as it was several hundred years ago.

Early History of Astronomy & Space

Humankind has studied the skies for centuries, seeking to find our place in the universe. Some of the most important discoveries in the field of astronomy were made in these texts recorded by ancient stargazers, but almost as impactful were the perspectives of those who considered their discoveries to be heresy. Any independent astronomer will find this an invaluable collection of titles arguing the truth of the cosmic system.

Early History of Industry & Science

Acting as a kind of historical Wall Street, this collection of industry manuals and records explores the thriving industries of construction; textile, especially wool and linen; salt; livestock; and many more.

Early English Wit, Poetry & Satire

The power of literary device was never more in its prime than during this period of history, where a wide array of political and religious satire mocked the status quo and poetry called humankind to transcend the rigors of daily life through love, God or principle. This series comments on historical patterns of the human condition that are still visible today.

Early English Drama & Theatre

This collection needs no introduction, combining the works of some of the greatest canonical writers of all time, including many plays composed for royalty such as Queen Elizabeth I and King Edward VI. In addition, this series includes history and criticism of drama, as well as examinations of technique.

Early History of Travel & Geography

Offering a fascinating view into the perception of the world during the sixteenth and seventeenth centuries, this collection includes accounts of Columbus's discovery of the Americas and encompasses most of the Age of Discovery, during which Europeans and their descendants intensively explored and mapped the world. This series is a wealth of information from some the most groundbreaking explorers.

Early Fables & Fairy Tales

This series includes many translations, some illustrated, of some of the most well-known mythologies of today, including Aesop's Fables and English fairy tales, as well as many Greek, Latin and even Oriental parables and criticism and interpretation on the subject.

Early Documents of Language & Linguistics

The evolution of English and foreign languages is documented in these original texts studying and recording early philology from the study of a variety of languages including Greek, Latin and Chinese, as well as multilingual volumes, to current slang and obscure words. Translations from Latin, Hebrew and Aramaic, grammar treatises and even dictionaries and guides to translation make this collection rich in cultures from around the world.

Early History of the Law

With extensive collections of land tenure and business law "forms" in Great Britain, this is a comprehensive resource for all kinds of early English legal precedents from feudal to constitutional law, Jewish and Jesuit law, laws about public finance to food supply and forestry, and even "immoral conditions." An abundance of law dictionaries, philosophy and history and criticism completes this series.

Early History of Kings, Queens and Royalty

This collection includes debates on the divine right of kings, royal statutes and proclamations, and political ballads and songs as related to a number of English kings and queens, with notable concentrations on foreign rulers King Louis IX and King Louis XIV of France, and King Philip II of Spain. Writings on ancient rulers and royal tradition focus on Scottish and Roman kings, Cleopatra and the Biblical kings Nebuchadnezzar and Solomon.

Early History of Love, Marriage & Sex

Human relationships intrigued and baffled thinkers and writers well before the postmodern age of psychology and self-help. Now readers can access the insights and intricacies of Anglo-Saxon interactions in sex and love, marriage and politics, and the truth that lies somewhere in between action and thought.

Early History of Medicine, Health & Disease

This series includes fascinating studies on the human brain from as early as the 16th century, as well as early studies on the physiological effects of tobacco use. Anatomy texts, medical treatises and wound treatment are also discussed, revealing the exponential development of medical theory and practice over more than two hundred years.

Early History of Logic, Science and Math

The "hard sciences" developed exponentially during the 16th and 17th centuries, both relying upon centuries of tradition and adding to the foundation of modern application, as is evidenced by this extensive collection. This is a rich collection of practical mathematics as applied to business, carpentry and geography as well as explorations of mathematical instruments and arithmetic; logic and logicians such as Aristotle and Socrates; and a number of scientific disciplines from natural history to physics.

Early History of Military, War and Weaponry

Any professional or amateur student of war will thrill at the untold riches in this collection of war theory and practice in the early Western World. The Age of Discovery and Enlightenment was also a time of great political and religious unrest, revealed in accounts of conflicts such as the Wars of the Roses.

Early History of Food

This collection combines the commercial aspects of food handling, preservation and supply to the more specific aspects of canning and preserving, meat carving, brewing beer and even candy-making with fruits and flowers, with a large resource of cookery and recipe books. Not to be forgotten is a "the great eater of Kent," a study in food habits.

Early History of Religion

From the beginning of recorded history we have looked to the heavens for inspiration and guidance. In these early religious documents, sermons, and pamphlets, we see the spiritual impact on the lives of both royalty and the commoner. We also get insights into a clergy that was growing ever more powerful as a political force. This is one of the world's largest collections of religious works of this type, revealing much about our interpretation of the modern church and spirituality.

Early Social Customs

Social customs, human interaction and leisure are the driving force of any culture. These unique and quirky works give us a glimpse of interesting aspects of day-to-day life as it existed in an earlier time. With books on games, sports, traditions, festivals, and hobbies it is one of the most fascinating collections in the series.

old books. new life.

The BiblioLife Network

This project was made possible in part by the BiblioLife Network (BLN), a project aimed at addressing some of the huge challenges facing book preservationists around the world. The BLN includes libraries, library networks, archives, subject matter experts, online communities and library service providers. We believe every book ever published should be available as a high-quality print reproduction; printed on-demand anywhere in the world. This insures the ongoing accessibility of the content and helps generate sustainable revenue for the libraries and organizations that work to preserve these important materials.

The following book is in the "public domain" and represents an authentic reproduction of the text as printed by the original publisher. While we have attempted to accurately maintain the integrity of the original work, there are sometimes problems with the original work or the micro-film from which the books were digitized. This can result in minor errors in reproduction. Possible imperfections include missing and blurred pages, poor pictures, markings and other reproduction issues beyond our control. Because this work is culturally important, we have made it available as part of our commitment to protecting, preserving, and promoting the world's literature.

GUIDE TO FOLD-OUTS MAPS and OVERSIZED IMAGES

The book you are reading was digitized from microfilm captured over the past thirty to forty years. Years after the creation of the original microfilm, the book was converted to digital files and made available in an online database.

In an online database, page images do not need to conform to the size restrictions found in a printed book. When converting these images back into a printed bound book, the page sizes are standardized in ways that maintain the detail of the original. For large images, such as fold-out maps, the original page image is split into two or more pages

Guidelines used to determine how to split the page image follows:

• Some images are split vertically; large images require vertical and horizontal splits.
• For horizontal splits, the content is split left to right.
• For vertical splits, the content is split from top to bottom.
• For both vertical and horizontal splits, the image is processed from top left to bottom right.

Iter Carolinum,

BEING

A Succinct RELATION

OF

The Neceffitated *Marches*, *Retreats*,

and *Sufferings*

Of His MAJESTY

CHARLS the I.

From *January* 10. 1 6 4 1. till the time of
His Death 1 6 4 8.

---

*Collected by a daily Attendant upon his Sacred
Majefty during all the faid time.*

LONDON,

Printed by *W. Godbid* over againft the *Anchor*
Inne in *Little Brittain.* 1 6 6 0.

To the Loyall Reader.

I Do here present thee with a compendious collection of thy late Soveraignes afflictions, which are many and unparallell'd, in so much that I may truly say, (though therein contradictory to the wise man, who saith, There is nothing new under the Sun) *that there was no such deed done or seen from the beginning of the world untill this day.*

Look not hereon, I conjure thee, unless with tears, nay indeed how canst thou? to see the King driven from place to place, affronted, neglected, despised, hungring, and thirsting, reviled, persecuted and defamed. So that he might justly take up that of the Apostle, 1 Cor. 4. 9, 10. &c. *And indeed* hinc fons ille lacrymarum ; *From this Fountain came all our future sorrows: This, this, I say, was the cause of our succeeding miseries, our inestimable loss and almost inexpiable ruine ; but* propitiatur Deus, *so infinite is God in his mercy that he not onely can but will pardon, though his justice severely denounceth this Sentence :* The soul that sins shall die.

A 2

But

To the Loyal Reader.

But our present time speaks better things. We have the pool of Bethesda, whereat many have lain groaning even despairing for help, and Now God hath sent his Angel and moved the water, and the whole Nation by stepping in, are healed of the disease they too too long laboured under : *O terque quaterque beatus!* Thrice happy he whose Loyal actings by Heaven have crowned been with such a blest success, that after times shall call him and confess he was his Countries Honor, and his Princes Shield. *Pardon I pray, good Reader, this zealous digression, and in the short ensuing Tractate please to take notice that it begins at the 10. of* Jan. 1641 *when his Majestie was forced by Tumults from* White-hall, *and is continued till his death after the manner of a* Diary, *pointing out his travel from place to place, with their distances from each other; his abode therein & entertainment, succinctly withal, yet mystically relating the most remarkable passages and battails occurring in that time. I need say no more, but let it speak for its self; I suppose there are many who will remember much thereof ; I know the Author my Father and Self were* Testes *oculati, speaking onely what we had sorrowfully seen and known.* Oh that Posterity may never know the like ! but for ever rest satisfied in their undoubted Soveraign, that his Generation may never fail to sway the *Scepter in these Kingdomes,* while the Sun and Moon endureth : *Which is the cordial prayer of his Majesties most faithfull Subject,*

THOMAS MANLEY.

A List of his Majesties marches and Removes since his coming from London, on Monday the tenth of January, Anno Dom. 1641.

January, 1641.

		Nights.	Miles.
10.	FRom *White-Hall* to *Hampton-Court* ———	ij	xij
12.	To *Windsor* ———————	xxviij	x

February.

9.	To *Hampton-Court*, riding somewhat out of the way ———	j	xij
10.	To *Greenwich* ———————	j	xiv
11.	To *Rochester* ———————	j	xx
12.	To *Canterbury* ———————	iv	xxij
16.	To *Dover* ———————	ix	xij
25.	The Queen went aboard to *Holland* in the *Lyon*.		

	Nights.	Miles.
25. To *Canterbury*	i	xij
26. To *Greenwich*	ii	xlii
28. To *Theobales*	iv	xvi

March.

3. To *Royston*	v	xxi
7. To *New-market*	v	xx
14. To *Huntington*	i	xxiv
15. To *Stanford*	i	xxi
16. To *Grantham*	i	xvi
17. To *Newarke*	i	x
18. To *Doncaster*	i	xxviii
19. To *York*	cx	xxviii

July, 1642. Lincolne Journey.

7. To *Beverley*	v	xxii
12. To *Doncaster*	i	xxviii
13. To *Newarke*	i	xxviii
14. To *Lincolne*	ii	xii
16. To *Beverley*	ii	xlv

Leicester Journey.

21. To *Nottingham*	i	lx
22. To *Leicester*	iv	xvi

26. To

	Nights.	Miles.
26. to *Doncaster*	i	xxxii
7. to *Beverley*	iii	xxviii
30. to *York*	xvii	xxii

August, 1642.

	Nights.	Miles.
16. to *Nottingham,* Earl of *Clare*	ii	lv
18. to *Leicester*	i	xvi
19. to *Stonely* Abbey Sir *Tho. Lee*	iii	xx
23. to *Nottingham* Earl of *Clare,* where his Majesty set up his Royal Standard	xxi	

September.

	Nights.	Miles.
13. to *Darby*	iii	xii
16. to *Utoxeter*	i	
17. to *Stafford*	ii	
19. to *Wellington*	i	
20. to *Shrewsbury*	iii	
23. to *Westchester*	iv	xxviii
27. to *Shrewsbury*	xv	xxvii

October.

	Nights.	Miles.
12. to *Bridgenorth*	iii	
15. to *Wolverhampton*	iii	x
17. to *Bremichem Afton,* Sir *Tho. Holts*	ii	
18. to *Packington,* Sir *Rob. Fishers*	i	

19. To

	Nights.	Miles.
19. To *Killingworth* ———	i	
21. To *Southam* ———	ii	x
22. To *Edgcott* ———	i	ix

Edgehill Battell.

23. *Octob.* The great Battell at *Edghill* was ſtricken, the Earl of *Lindſey* General for his Majeſty, who was kill'd in the Fleld; and his Majeſty, notwithſtanding the Treachery of his chiefe Gunner, the loſſe and retaking his Standard, with the death of Sir *Edmund Verney*, the over-eager purſuit of the Parliaments wing of Horſe, by Prince *Rupert*, (whoſe Soldiers too ſoon fell to Plunder) remained ſole Maſters of the Field, and the next day had the Plunder of the Field.

	Nights.	Miles.
26. To *Aynow* on the Hill———	iv	x
28. To *Woodſtock* ———	ii	x
29. To *Oxford* ———	iv	vi

November.

	Nights.	Miles.
3. To *Benſon* ———	i	x
4. To *Reading* ———	iv	x
8. To *Maidenhead* ———	ii	
10. To *Colebrook*	ii	
12. To *Hownſlow* ———	ii	v

Brainford Fight.

After *Edgehil* battle, his Majeſtie having continued his marching as aforeſaid towards *London* in
the way at *Brainford*, fell upon ſome Forces of the
Parliaments there, falling into their Quarters, and
with much courage putting them to the worſt, till
relieved by other Regiments lying near it, became
a hot fight in the fields, lanes and ſtreets: His Majeſties forces ſtill valiantly maintaining their ground
they had at firſt got, untill by intelligence nnder-
ſtanding the vaſt ſupplies both of horſe and foot
that were coming out of *London* ; finding it impoſ-
ſible to be abſolute Victors, it was thought fit to
retreat with honour and ſafetie, which they did,
marching away through *Kingſton*

Nights, Miles.

		Nights	Miles
13.	To *Hampton* Court ———	i	
14.	To *Oatlands* ———	i	iv
18.	To *Bagſhott* ———	iv	viii
19.	To *Reading*, which immediately upon the Kings receſs was ſurren-dred to the Earl of *Eſſex* ———	ix	x
29.	To *VVallingford* dinner, *Oxford* ſupper, and there during pleaſure ———		

Novem-

November 1644.

A Lift of his Majefties Marches from Oxford to Briftol, Glocefter *Siege, &c. Beginning the* 1. *of* Auguft 1643.

Nights, Miles.

1 From *Oxford* to *Farrindon* dinner, to *Malmesbury* fupper and bed-- } j xij xvj

Briftow taken by the King.

2. To *Briftow* ———— vj xxij
8. To *Tedbury* dinner, to *Cirencefter* fupper and bed, Sir *William Mafters* ———— } j xx viij
9. To *Panfweek* ———— j xj

Glocefter befieged.

10. To *Macfeon,* Mr. *Selwins* near *Glocefter* ———— } xxvj iv

September.

5. To *Panfweek* ——— j iiv
6. To *Bantley-Hill* dinner, to *Coverley* fupper and bed ——— } j viij
7. Diner in the field, to *Sudeley* Caftle fupper and bed ——— } iv xij
11. Diner in the field, to *Evifholme* fupper and bed ——— } j xiv
12. To *Parfhall* ij iv

The

The *Earl* of *Essex* approaching with his
Army, the *King* raised his Siege from
Glocester, and marched--

		Nights,	Miles.
14. To *Evisham* ———		ij	iv
16. To *Snowes* hill———		j	vj
17. To *Norlich*, dinner, *Alscoc* supper——		j	xij
18. To *Faringdon* dinner, to *VVantage* Sir *George Wilmots* supper and bed—		j	x
19. Diner in the field *Newbery*, to supper and bed Mr. *Coxes*, and on Wednesday the 20. the great battle was struck there———		iv	x
23. To *Oxford* ——— during pleasure —			xx

April 1644.

		Nights,	Miles.
9. From *Oxford* to *Childrey* the Lady *Fetiplace* ——		j	xij
10. To *Marlingborow* the Lord *Seymers*-		j	xiij
11. To *VVantage* diner, to *Oxford* supper and bed—during pleasure ——		xv	x

May 1644.

		Nights,	Miles.
16. To *Coley* near *Reading* ———		ij	xxij
18. Diner to *Compton*, *Oxford* supper and bed —during pleasure———		xij	xiij

A List

A List of his Majesties March with his Armies towards the West, &c. Beginning on Sonday the 2. of June, An. Dom. 1644.

June 1644.

Nights Miles.

SUnday the 2. day, in the afternoon we went from *Oxford*, to *Woodstock*, and returned back that night on Monday morning the 3. day about 6. a clock his Majesty came back again to *Oxford* ———   j   vj

Monday the 3. day, and Tuesday the 4. About 9. a clock at night his Majesty marched again to *Woodstock* ward, but left it on the right hand ; to *Burford* to supper; the 4. day, and that night lodged at *Burton* on on the water at Doctor *Temples* ———   ij   xviij

Wednesday the 5. to *Evisham*, Mr. Alderman *Martins* ———   i   xv

Thursday the 6. to *Worcester* the Bishops Pallace ———   vi   xij

Tuesday

	Nights,	Miles.
Tuesday the 12. to *Bewdley*, Sir Thomas *Littletons* ———	iii	xii
Saturday the 15. to *VVorcester* again, the Bishops Pallace ———	i	xii
Sunday the 16. to *Bradway*, Mistris *Savages* ———	i	xvii
Monday the 17. to *Burford*, the *George* ———	i	xii
Tuesday the 18. to *Witney*, the *white Hart* ———	iii	vi
Friday the 21. to *Blechenton*, Sir Thomas *Coghils* ———	i	vii
Saturday the 22. to *Buckingham*, Sir *Thomas Richardsons* ———	iv	xii
Wednesday the 26. to *Brackley* the Colledge there ———	i	ii
Thursday the 27. to *Culworth*, Sir Samuel *Danvers* ———	i	viii
Friday the 28. to *Grymsbury*, a Yeomans house ———	i	vii
Saturday the 29. to *Williamscot*, a very poor mans house ———	ii	iv

July 1644.

| Monday the 1. to *Dedington*, the Parsonage ——— | i | ii |

C

Tuesday

	Nights.	Miles.
Tuesday the 2. to *Morton Hinmarch*, the *white Hart* ———	i	xii
Wednesday the 3. to *Evisham*, Alderman *Martins* ———	ix	x
Friday the 12. to *Coverley* the E. of *Downes*, by *Bradway* and *Sudeley* ——	i	xvi
Saturday the 13. to *Sapperton*, Sir *Henry Pooles* near *Cirencester* ——	i	vii
Sunday the 14. to *Bodmyngton*, the Lo. *Herbets* of *Ragland* ———	i	xiv
Monday the 15. to *Bath*, Sir *Thomas Bridges* the Governors ———	ii	xi
Wednesday the 17. to *Mells*, sir *John Horners* the Kings by attainder——	ii	viii
Friday the 19. to *Bruton*, sir *Charles Bartleys* ———	ii	x
Saturday the 20. to *Ilchester*, Master *Dawes* house ———	iv	xii
Wednesday the 24. to *Charde*, Master *Barcrofts* a Merchant of *London* --	i	xii
Thursday the 25. to *Hunington*, Doctor *Marwoods* a Phisitian ———	i	xii
Friday the 26. to *Excester Bedford houf*, sir *John Bartleys* the Governonr——	i	xv
Saturday the 27. to *Crediton* diner ; to *Bradinch*, Mr. *Seuters* supper——	i	xvi
Sunday the 28. to *Crediton*, Master *Tuckers* house———	i	viii

Monday

		Nights	Miles
Monday the 29. to *Bow*, Mr. *Philips* a mean quarter———		i	x
Tuesday the 30. to *Oachampton*, at Mr. *Rotenburies*———		i	viii
Wednesday the last, to *Lifton* the Parsonage house———		i	viii

August 1644.

		Nights	Miles
Thursday the first, to *Trecarroll* Mr. *Maningtons* house in *Cornwall*———		i	ix
Friday the 2. to *Liskerd* Mr. *Jeane* a Commissioners house———		vi	viii
Thursday the 8. to *Boconnock* the Lord *Mohuns*, but called from thence to make ready at Mr. *Glins* of *Glinford*, affrighted from thence by the *Militia*, his Majestie lay in the field all night in his Coach on *Boconnock* Downe a Heathy place———		i	v
Friday the 9. to *Boconnock* again, where his Majesty quartered———		xxi	v
Saturday the last day, to *Leftithiall*, thence toward *Foy*, his Majesty lay in the field his meat and drink dreft at M. *Hixts*, the *Militia* disarmed, E. fled the field, the Articles confirmd.		ii	v

Nights, Miles.

And here his Majesties Clemency was
moſt Eminent, when having all the
Infantry at his mercy, he not onely
pardoned the Souldiers in general,
but admitted the chief Officers to   ii   v
kiſs his hand, onely refuſed that fa-
vour to M. G. *Skippon*, as being too
great an enemy to his Majesties Honour and ſafety.———————

September 1644.

Monday the 2. to *Becennock* the Lord   ii   v
Mohuns again———————

Wedneſday the 4. to *Liskerd* Maſter   i   vii
Jeanes ———————

Thurſday the 5. to *Taviſtock*, the La-   v   xv
dy *Glanvils*———————

Tueſday the 10. to *Widey* near *Ply-*   iv   x
mouth, yeoman *Heales* houſe———

Saturday 14. to *Taviſtock*, the Lady   iii   x
Glanvils———————

Monday the 16. to *Oakehampton*, Mr.   i   xii
Rottenburies ———————

Tueſday

Tuesday the 17. to *Excester*, *Bed-ford* house the Governours, at *Cre-diton*   vi   x x

Monday the 23. to *Chard*, Mr. *Barcrofts* at *Honiton* dinner   vii   x x vii

Monday the last day to *South Parrat*, Mr. *Gibs* dinner in the field   i   viii

October 1644.

Tuesday the 1. to *Mayden Newton*, Mr. *Osbornes* dinner in the field   i   viii

Wednesday the 2. to *Sherborn* lodge the Lord *Digbies* dinner in the field   vi   xii

Tuesday the 8. to *Stalbridge* the E. of *Corks* dined there   i   v

Wednesday the 9. to *Stirmister New-ton*, Mr. *Reeves* dinner in the field   i   iii

Thursday the 10. to *Brignstone* near *Blanford*, Mrs. *Rogers*   iv   vii

Monday the 14. to *Cranborn* lodge the E. of *Salisburies*, dinner in the field   i   x

Tuesday the 15. to *Salisbury*, D. *Sadlers* Chancelor, dinner in a little Lodge   iii   x

Friday the 18. to *Andiver* the *White Hart*, dinner in the field   i   x v

Saturday the 19. to *Whitchurch*, Mr. *Brookes* dinner in the field   ii   vii

Monday the 21. to *Kings Cleer*, Mr. Towers dinner at *VVhitchurch* —— i   v

Yet his *Majesties* March from the *West* in *October*.

October 1644.

Tuesday the 22. to *New-bury*, Master *Dunce*, dinner at *Kings Cleer* —— v.   vi

Sunday the 7. a great and second battel betwixt his Majesties Army, and the Parliaments, by the same hands his Majestie had disarm'd and shown mercy to at *Lestichiel*, wherein his Majestie had much the better of the day, & yet was advised to desert the field, whereby —— &c. His Majestie marched to meet Prince *Rupert* at Bathe, Prince *Maurice*, General *Goring*, and most of his Majesties houshold about 9. a clock that Sunday night marched from *Denyngton* Castle to *VVallingford*, and the next day Monday the 28. came all to *Oxford*, waiting for his Majestie —— i   xxv

His

His Majesties remarch from Bath *to* Oxford.

Nights, Miles.

Sonday the 27.from *Denington* Caftle
  marching all night,and on Monday } ii   I
  the 28.came to *Bath*,and there ——
Wednefday the 30. to *Churchfton* a }
  widowes houfe——— } i
Thurfday laft, to *Cirencefter*, Sir VVil- }
  liam Mafters Baronet ——— } i   xxvi

November 1644.

Friday the firft,to *Oxford* fupper, and there during
  pleafure.

A Lift of his Majefties Marches from Oxford *towards* Denyngton Caftle, *both to relieve it, and to draw off the Ordinance left there the 27. of* October *before.*

Wednefday the 6. to *Bullington* green
  the Randes vouz dinner, *Oxford*
  fupper, where P. R. was declared } ii   i
  General with great acclamation ——

                                                Thurfday

Thurſday the 7. to *VVallingford* Collonel *Blagues* the Governour ——— xii i

Friday the 8. to Weſt *Illeſley* the
Biſhop of *Gloceſter in comendum* — viii i

Saturday the 9. to *Denington* Caſtle
where was a great skirmiſh with the
Parliamentires in *Newbury* field,
whence we retreat ' ——ˡ lay on the
Caſtle all night ——— viii i

November. 1644.

Sonday the 10. to *Lamborn* Mr. *Gar-*
rets ——— viii ii

Tueſday the 12. to *Marlingborough* the
Lord *Seymers* ——— viii v

Sonday the 17. to *Hungerford* the
Bear ——— viii ii

Tueſday the 19. to *Shelford,* Maſter
Brownes, The Kings birth-day —— vi ii

Thurſday the 21. to *Charlton* near
VVantage, Sir *George VVilmot* —— vi i

Friday the 22. to *Farington,* Sir *Ro-*
bert Pyes ——— vii ii

Saturday the 23. to *Oxford* dinner, and
there during pleaſure ——— xiv all
(winter

A Liſt

Anno xxi. Regis Caroli, *May*.

A List of his Majesties several Marches, beginning upon Wednesday the vij. of May, Anno Dom. 1645.

	Nights,	Miles.
WEdnesday the 7. From *Oxford* *Woodstock* ————	i	vi
Thursday the 8. to *Stow* ith wole, Master *Jones* ———	i	xiii
Friday the 9. to *Evisholme,* Alderman *Martins* ———	i	xii
Saturday the 10. to *Inkeborow,* the Vicaridge ———	i	vi
Sonday the 11. to *Droitwicth* Master *Barrets* ———	iii	ix
Wednesday the 14. to *Cofton-hall,* Mrs. *skinners,Hawkesley-house* taken by *P.M.*in our march a Garrison ——	i	x
Thursday the 15. to *Hemly* near *Wolverhampton,* Mr. *Wars* ———	i	xii
Friday the 16. to *Bishberry* near *Sturbridge,*Mr.*Grosvenors* ———	i	vi
Saturday the 17.to *Chetwin* near *Newport,* Mr. *Pigots* ———	iii	xi. i
Tuesday the 20. to *Beaton* near *Drayton,* Mr. *Churches* ———	ii	viii

D   Thursday

	Nights.	Miles.
Thursday the 22. to *Park-hall* near *stone*, Mr. *Cromptons* ———	ii	x
Saturday the 24. to *Eaton* ith *Clay*, Sir *Tho. Millwares* ———	i	x
Sonday the 26. to *Tutbury* dinner, Lord *Loughborow* ———	ii	vi
Tuesday the 27. to *Asbby de la zonch* E. of *Huntingdons* ———	i	ix
Wednesday the 28. to *Coats* near *Loughborow*, Sir *H. Skipwiths* ———	i	ix
Thursday the 29. Remarched to *Elstone* near *Leicester*, which we faced with Souldiers, the R. defaced with fire ———	ii	x
Saturday the last, to *Leicester*, which was taken by his Majesty at 2 *mane* souldiers rewarded with the plunder, the slane equal on both sides, the Countess of *Devonshire* we demolished with fire ———	iv	iii

June 1645.

	Nights.	Miles.
Wednesday the 4. to *Wistow*, Sir *Richard Halfords* ———	i	v
Thursday the 5. to *Lubenham* near *Harborow*, Mr. *Collins* ———	ii	vii
Saturday the 7. to *Daventree* the *Wheat sheaf* from whence *Oxford* was relieved from a siege, and victualled--	vi	xiv

Friday

Friday the 13. Remarched again to *Lubnam*, Mr. *Collins* ———   i   xiv

Saturday the 14. An alarum afrighted the King and Army from *Lubnam* at 2 a clock in the morning to *Harborow* the Generals quarter, thence about 7 towards *Naseby*, where the Parliaments Army quartered, rashly fought with them, were utterly defeated through the cowardize of the horse, which fled to the walls of *Leicester* 16. miles, never faced nor rallied till there, whereby many of the horse, all the foot were either slain or taken prisoners, with some of his Majesties servants, all the Ordinance, Amunition, the Kings stuffe, Houshold-carriages, and all the Baggage of the Army were totally lost, the Parliament having the clearest victory given them from the begining; the King himself in person being necessitated, with his own troop only to charge through their body for his escape; from *Leicester* we marched to *Ashby de la zouch* in the night, and came thither about break of day, and halted there ——   i   xxviij

D 2   Sonday

Nights, Miles.

	Nights	Miles
Saturday the 15 to *Lichfield*, the Governours in the clofe ——	i	xij
Monday the 16 to *VVolverhampton*, Mrs. *Barnfords* a Widow ——	i	xij
Tuefday the 17 to *Bewdley* the Angel ——	ii	xiii
Thurfday the 19 to *Bramyard* dinner, to *Harriford* fupper——	xii	xxiv

July 1645.

	Nights	Miles
Tuefday the firft, to *Campfon* dinner Mr. *Pritchards*, to *Abergeveny* fupper, Mr. *Guncers*.———	iii	xv
Thurfday the 3 to *Ragland* fupper, Marquis of *Worcefter*——	xii	vii
Wednefday the 16 to *Tredeger* dinner, *Cardiffe* fupper Sir *T. Tirrels* defraid at the Countreyes charge	i	xx
Thurfday the 17 to *Tredegar*, Sir *VVilliam Morgans* to bed ——	i	viii

Friday

Friday the 18 to *Ragland* dinner, *&c.*
On Tuesday the 22 to Mr. *Moores*
of the Creek near Black-rock, and
came back to *Ragland*, supper but
came in so late as made us doubtful
of his majesties return; the *Scots* ap-
proach, and ourown causeless appre-
hension of fear, made us both demur
and doubt, on the first what to re-
solve, and in the latter how to steer
our resolutions, which involved us in
a most disasterous condition, *&c.*   vi   xii

Thursday the 24. From *Ragland* to Mr.
Mores of the Creek to pass over at
the black-rock for *Bristoll*, but his
Majestie sitting in councel, and ad-
vising to the contrary, marched only
with his own servants and troop,
that night to *Newport* on *Uske* lay
at Mistris *Pritties* ·   i   xxi

Yet his *Majesties* March in *July*, 1645.

Friday the 25 to *Rupperra*, Sir *Philip* *Morgans*   iv   v
Tuesday the 29 to *Cardiffe* dinner, the Governours at our own charge   vii   vii

August

August 1645.

Tuefday the 5 to *Glancayah* Mr. *Prit-chers* dinner, at *Bretknock* the Gover-nour, fupper —————— i   xxix

Wednefday the 6 to *Gurnevit* Sir *Hen-ry Williams*, dinner to old *Radnor* fupper a yeomans houfe, the Court difperfed —————— i   xviii

Thurfday the 7 to *Ludlow* Caftle no dinner, Col. *Woodhoufe* —————— i   xiv

Friday the great faft the 8 to *Bridge-north*, Sir *Lewis Kirkes* the Gover-nours —————— i   xiv

Sonday the 10 dinner near *Wolverhamp-ton in campis*, at *Lichfield* fupper the Governours in the clofe —————— ii   xxii

Tuefday the 12. to *Tutbury* caftle pr. in camp. and lying at the Lord *Lough-brows* —————— i   xii

Wednefday the 13 *Afhborn* i'th Peake, Mrs *Cakaines* —————— i   xiv

Thurfday the 14 to *Chattisford* near *Bakewell*, E. of *Devonfhires* —————— i   xiv

Friday the 15 to *Welbeck* Marquefs of *Newcaftles* —————— ii   xii

Monday the 17 to *Edlington* Mafter *Bofviles* —————— i   xi

Monday

Nights, Miles.

Monday the 18 day, to *Doncaster* the three Cranes ——— ii   ii*i*

Wednesday the 20 to *Redford*, master *Lane* a Lawyer —— i   xiv

Thursday the 21 to *Newark* the Lord *Danecourtes* ——— i   xiv

Friday the 22 to *Belvoyre* the E. of *Rut-lands* ——— i   xii

Saturday the 23 to *Stanford* the George ——— i   xii

Sonday the 24 to *Huntington* the George ——— i   xvi

Monday the 26 to *Woborn* the E. of *Bedfords* —— ii   xxi

Wednesday the 27 to *Ascot* near *Winge* E. *Carnarvous* —— i   xx

Thursday the 28 to *Oxford* at *Christ-Church* and there ——— ii   xx

A second List of his Majesties Marches from Oxford *on* Saturday the 30 *of* August, 1645.

SAturday the 30 to *Morton Hin* the March *white Hart* ——— i   xxiv

Sonday the last, no dinner, supper at *Worcester,* a cruel day —— iii   xxiv

August

September 1645.

Wednesday the 3 to *Bramyard*, Miſtris
Baynhams ——— } i   x

Thurſday the 4 to *Hereford* dinner Bi-
ſhops Pallace ——— } i   x

Friday the 5 to *Lempſter* dinner at the
Unicorn, to *Webley* ſupper the *Unicorn* } i   xiv

Saturday the 6 to *Hereford* dinner Bi-
ſhops Pallace ——— } i   vii

Sonday the 7 to *Ragland* caſtle ſupper,
17. Monday, the 8 to *Abergain* dinner,
Ragland ſupper, 14. Thurſday the 11
to *Ragland* ſupper, *Abergeveny* dinner 14 ——— } vii   xlv

Sonday the 14 to *Monmouth* dinner
the Governours, to *Hereford* ſupper, monday the 15 we marched
half way to *Bramyard*, but there was
Leo in itinere, and ſo back to *Hereford*
again ——— } iii   x

Wedneſday the 18. the *Randezvous*
was at *Athurſtone* there dined, 10
miles, to *Hamlacy* ſupper, Lord *Scu-
dainores* ——— } i   xxvi

Thurſday

Nights. Miles.

Thurſday the 18 to a *Randezvouz* 5 miles from *Hamlacy*, with intention for *Worceſter*, *Poins* and *Roſceſter* in the paſſage, whereupon we remarched towards *Hereford*, ſo to *Lempſter*, then to *VVebley*, thence to *Preſtine*, there halted at maſter *Andrewes* ; this march laſted from 6 in the morning, till midnight, *&c.*   i   x x viii

Friday the 19 to *Newtown* Mr. *Price*, a long march over the mountains · —   ii   xiv

Sonday the 21 to *Llanvillin* ſupper, dinner Mr. *Prices* ——   i   x x

Monday the 22 to *Chirke* caſtle, ſir *Jo. VVats* the governours ——   i   xiv

Tueſday 23 to *Llangollen* 4. to *Wrixham* 8 to *Cheſter* ; a great fight between *Cheſter* and *Tarvin*, the King Victor, but made no uſe of it, leaving *Cheſter* unreleaved. This was performed by the ſame horſe that fled at *Naſeby* on *Rowton* Heath againſt Coll. *Poyntz*, and the Army under his command ——   ii   xx

Thurſday the 25. dinner at *Cheſter*, march'd to *Hawarden* Caſtle, halted there thence, to *Northop*, to *Skiviock*, to *Potvary*, to *Denbigh*, *Will.Salſb.* of *Bohumbed* Governor —,   iii   x x

E   Son-

<table>
<tr><td></td><td>Nights.</td><td>Miles.</td></tr>
<tr><td>Sonday the 28 dinner at Denbigh, supper late at Chirke castle———</td><td>i</td><td>xviii</td></tr>
<tr><td>Monday the 29 dinner at Chirk castle, supper at Halton in Mongomery-shire Master Lloyds———</td><td>i</td><td>xxvi</td></tr>
<tr><td>Tuesday the last, prand. in camp. supper at Bridgnorth the Governors———</td><td>ii</td><td>xxx</td></tr>
</table>

October 1645.

<table>
<tr><td>Thursday the 2 dinner at Ridgheath, the Randezvouz, supper at Lichfield the Close———</td><td>i</td><td>xxii</td></tr>
<tr><td>Friday the 3 no dinner, at Tongue supper Mr. Suttons———</td><td>i</td><td>xv</td></tr>
<tr><td>Saturday the 4 no dinner, at Newarke supper Lord Danecourts ———</td><td>ix</td><td>xxvi</td></tr>
<tr><td>Sonday the 12 to Tuxfords the white Hart ———</td><td>i</td><td>xii</td></tr>
<tr><td>Monday the 13 dinner in the field, at Welbeck supper Marquiss Newcastle-</td><td>i</td><td>xii</td></tr>
<tr><td>Tuesday the xiv. no dinner at Newarke, supper Lord Danecourts———</td><td>xviii</td><td>xii</td></tr>
</table>

November

November 1645.

Monday the 3 day of *November*, *Anno Dom*. 1645. His Majeſtie about a 11 a clock at night, went out of *Newark*, marched all that night, all the next day being Tueſday at 12 a clock that night, halted at *Codsbury*, Wedneſday about 10 a clock in the morning came to *Banbury*, made an halt and dined there at the caſtle, and afterward the ſame Wedneſday the 5 of *November* about 5 a clock in the Evening came to *Oxford* to ſupper, and continued there during pleaſure ———   iv   xc

His Majeſtie went from *Oxford* the 27 of *April* 1646. towards *Newark* to the *Scottiſh* Leaguer there, but in regard of the privateneſs of his going away, *Oxford* being at that time beleagured by Sir *Thomas Fairfax* his Army, and the fewneſs of his attendants, being at the moſt but two, we have no certaintie where he ſtayed by the way, but ſhortly after he appeared in the *Scots* Army, who pretended to protect him from his *Engliſh* Rebbels and for the better ſecuring his Majeſties Perſon from dan-

    ger

ger as was pretended they stayed not long after
at *Newarke*, but by easie marches removed with
his Majesties Person from *Newarke* to *Newcastle*,
where the solemne Argument between his said
Majestie and Master *Henderson* happened con-
cerning Episcopasie, and Church Government,
to his Majesties everlasting Honour. But such
was the horrid perfidy of those Treacherous *Scots*,
that in stead of the expected safetie of his Majesties Person, *Judas* like for money, (though a
far greater summe) sold and delivered their Soveraign L O R D and K I N G, into the hands
of his *English* Rebels, who by this means had
under God a power to resettle the Kingdomes
Peace: But they were blinded to their own de-
struction; and having taken the Lords Annointed
in their pits, they now used him as they listed,
carried him whither they pleased, and indeed
treated him no otherwise then as their Prisoner,
for with a strong Guard of Horse and Foot in
the moneth of *February* 1646. the depth of
Winter, they begin to remove him from *Newcastle* in manner following:

His

His Majesties Gests from New-castle *to* Holdenby *in* Februarie 1646.

	Nights.	Miles.
3 DAy from *Newcastle* to *Durham*	i	xii
4 From thence, to *Aukeland*	i	
5 From thence, to *Richmond*	i	
6 From thence, to *Rippon*	ii	
8 From thence, to *VVakefield*	i	
9 From thence, to *Rotheram*	i	
10 From thence, to *Mansfield*	i	
11 From thence, to *Nottingham*	i	xii
12 From thence, to *Leicester*	i	xvi
13 From thence, to *Holdenby*	dur. plea.	

Long

Long had not his Sacred Majeftie continued there, but he was by a part of the Army under one *Joyce*, violently taken from thence, and brought to his Honor of *Hampton Court* ; where for a while he feemed to begin to reaffume his Priftine Majefty; being admitted to fee and to be feen ; but *Cromwell* fearing the frequencie of fo great refort might fpoil his Trayterous defigns with much Serpentine craft and devillifh fubtiltie, perfwaded and infinuated into his Majefties heart doubts and fufpitions of mifchief intended againft him ; the onely way for preventing whereof, he affirmed to be the withdrawing his Perfon from thence, to a place of more ftrength and fecurity, and to that purpofe nominated the *Ifle* of *VVight*, to which place his Majefty led by the Innocency of his fpotlefle Confcience, was decoyed, and at his arrival found himfelf over-reached ; for he was immediately fecured by Collonel *Hammond*, who then wa Governor in the faid *Ifland*, and kept a long time a prifoner there in the Caftle of *Carisbrook* ; until afterwards, upon the Petitions of moft Counties o *England* , a perfonal Treatie was appointed to b held in the faid *Ifle* at *Newport*, for which end Commiffioners were fent thither with Inftructions, an the Treatie begun, and profecuted with fo goo effect, that his Majefties Conceffions at that time were voted by the Parliament a fufficient groun to proceed on for the fettlement of the Peace o of the Kingdome. But here again, his Majeftie is violently and trayterouſly ſeized by the Army then under *Fairfax* his command; by whom *December* the firſt, 1648. He was brought to *Hurſt* Caſtle in *Hampſhire*, and there kept as a priſoner, till the 21. of the ſame moneth, when he was brought to *VVincheſter*, thence the 23. to *Windſor*, where for little time he ſtayed, attended by ſtrong Guards of ſouldiers, till about the 9. of *January* following; when they removed him towards *London*, and brought him to his own Houſe at Saint *James*'s, and conſequently to perfidious *London*, (Oh infortunate Monarch!) where not long after with helliſh effrontery even in deſpight of Heaven, at noon Day before His own Houſe *VVhitehall*, in the open ſtreet with armed multitudes of ſouldiers, they Sacrilegiouſly murthered that Bleſſed though unfortunate Prince) C H A R L E S the Firſt;

There being actually guilty of that horrid murther, by giving Sentence, and ſigning the warrant for his beheading.

John Bradſhaw, Preſident.	Lord Gray of Groby,
John Liſle,	Sir *John Danvers* Knight,
William Say,	Sir *Thomas Maleverer* Bar.
Oliver Cromwel,	Sir *John Bourchier* Knight.
Henry Ireton,	*William Heueningham*,
Sir *Hardreſſe Waller*,	Alderman *Pennington*,
Valentine Walton,	*William Purefoy*,
Thomas Harriſon,	*Henry Martin*,
Edward Whaley,	*John Barkſtead*,
Thomas Pride,	*John Blackiſton*,
Iſaac Ewers,	*Gilbert Millington*,

Sir

Sir William Constable Bar.
Edmond Ludlow,
John Hutchinson,
Sir Mich. Livesey Bar.
Robert Titchbourne,
Owen Roe,
Robert Lilburn,
Adrian Scroop,
Richard Deane,
John Okey,
John Hewson,
William Goffe,
Cornelius Holland,
John Carey,
John Jones,
Miles Corbet,
Francis Allin,
Peregrine Pelham,
John Moore,
John Aldred,
Henry Smith,
Humphrey Edwards,

Gregory Clement,
Thomas Woogan,
Sir Gregory Norton Knight.
Edmond Harvy,
John Venn,
Thomas Scot,
Thomas Andrews Alderman,
William Cawly,
Anthony Stapley,
John Downes,
Thomas Horton
Thomas Hammond,
Nicholas Love,
Vincent Potter,
Augustine Garland,
John Dixwel.
George Fleetwood,
Symon Meyne,
James Temple,
Peter Temple,
Daniel Blagrave,
Thomas Waite.

Councellors Assistant to the Court, and to draw up the Charge against the King; Dr. Dorislaus, Mr. Aske, Mr. Steel Attorney General, Mr. Cook Sollicitor General, Mr. Broughton, Mr. Phelps Clerks to the Court.

Officers of the Court.

Sergeant Dandy Sergeant at Arms, Collonel Humphrey Sword-bearer.

Messengers, Dore-keepers and Criers, were these, viz.

Mr. Walford, Mr. Radley, Mr. Pain, Mr. Powel, Mr. Hull, Mr. King.

Sir Hardress Waller, Coll. Harrison Commissary Genenerall Ireton, Coll. Deane, and Coll. Okey, appointed the place to be the street before White-hall, and the time the 30. of January.

F I N I S.

Lightning Source UK Ltd.
Milton Keynes UK
UKHW02f1011180718
325892UK00007B/637/P